George Washington Carver

Agriculture Pioneer

Stephanie Macceca

Life Science Readers:
George Washington Carver
Agriculture Pioneer

Publishing Credits

Editorial Director
Dona Herweck Rice

Creative Director
Lee Aucoin

Associate Editor
Joshua BishopRoby

Illustration Manager
Timothy J. Bradley

Editor-in-Chief
Sharon Coan, M.S.Ed.

Publisher
Rachelle Cracchiolo, M.S.Ed

Science Contributor
Sally Ride Science™

Science Consultants
Thomas R. Ciccone, B.S., M.A.Ed.
    Chino Hills High School
Dr. Ron Edwards,
    DePaul University

Teacher Created Materials Publishing

5301 Oceanus Drive
Huntington Beach, CA 92649-1030
http://www.tcmpub.com
ISBN 978-0-7439-0590-9

Table of Contents

George Washington Carver

George Washington Carver was born a slave in 1864. After the Civil War, he became an important scientist. He was the first black man to receive a graduate degree in agriculture.

Carver was a skilled **botanist**. He became famous for his work with peanuts and other plants. He used them to make new products. Carver was also a great teacher. He taught both students and farmers **crop-rotation** methods. That meant they would change the crops they planted each season. It let the soil rest between plantings to keep it healthy.

Carver was a great scientist, but he was humble, too. He was offered a lot of money for his discoveries. But he never accepted it. He believed the plants and their secrets belonged to everyone.

George Washington Carver in 1915

Many Uses for the Peanut
Carver may be best known for the detailed and amazing work he did with the peanut. He found over 300 uses for it!

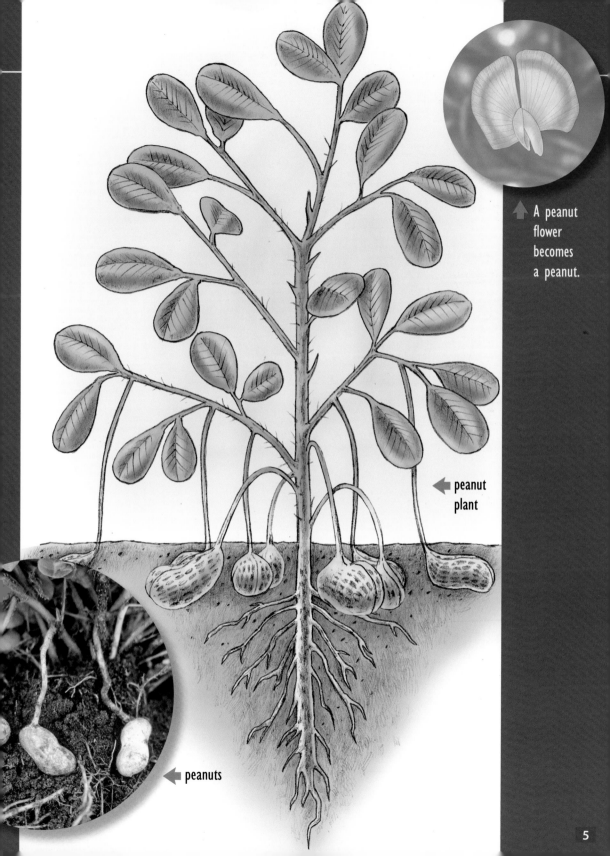

A peanut
flower
becomes
a peanut.

peanut
plant

peanuts

Born a Slave

Carver had a brother named Jim. Their mother's name was Mary, and she was a slave. She was bought by a German couple named Moses and Susan Carver. They did not approve of slavery, but still they used slaves as workers for their farm. The Carvers treated Mary and her children well, though.

Slave raiders kidnapped Carver and his mother when he was just an infant. John Bentley, the Carvers' neighbor, took the job of finding them. Moses offered a reward for their safe return. He would give 40 acres of prime **timberland** and one of his racehorses.

Slaves were used to harvest cotton and other crops.

What Is an *Abolitionist*?

For many years, slavery was legal in North America. **Abolitionists** were people who believed that slavery was wrong and should be illegal. The word comes from *abolish*, which means to destroy. That's what they wanted to do to slavery.

A Big Reward

The reward Moses Carver offered for finding his slaves was worth $1,100. That was a lot of money for the time!

Carver was found abandoned along the road in Arkansas. He was more dead than alive. His mother was not found. Carver and his brother had no living relatives. So the Carvers raised them as their own children. Carver was sickly and weak. He could not do work in the fields. So, he helped with the laundry, cooked, and learned to sew.

Frederick Douglass was a well-known abolitionist.

Segregation meant that white people and black people were kept separate, as on this bus.

Early Education

The Carvers tried to send the boys to a local school. They were turned away because they were black. The schools in Missouri were **segregated.**

Carver finally started school when he was about 11 years old. He walked eight miles to get there. He arrived too late in the night to find a room with a family. So he slept in a barn.

Carver moved in with the childless black couple who owned the barn. He helped them by doing household chores.

Carver was curious about nature. He collected **specimens** of many plants and insects. He **experimented** with the soil. He wanted to find out what the best soil was for each kind of plant. He saw that plants have an internal plumbing system. It brings water and **nutrients** from the soil to the leaves.

Herbs Used for Medicines

yarrow

chamomile

dandelion

feverfew

wild chicory

No Resources
Carver's childhood house had few books in it. In fact, when he was growing up, there were only two books in the house. They were *Webster's Elementary Spelling Book* and the Bible.

The Plant Doctor
Young Carver often helped his neighbors with their sick plants. He would nurse them back to health. As a child, he was a natural at botany. So he was nicknamed "The Plant Doctor."

Young Herbalist
The lady that Carver lived with taught him which herbs and plants could be used as medicine. She was a **midwife**. That is a person who delivers babies. She also took care of sick people.

Elizabeth Britton (1858–1934)

Elizabeth Britton was born in New York City. She was the oldest of five daughters. Her family moved to Cuba. There she was raised on a sugar plantation. She was able to go to school both in Cuba and in New York. She did especially well in her science classes.

Britton studied botany. She graduated from a college called the Normal School. Afterward, she worked there. She was very interested in moss. Although she did not have an advanced degree, she became a leading expert in the field.

After she married a college professor, Britton was put in charge of the moss collection at Columbia University. She also worked to preserve wildflowers. She helped start the New York Botanical Garden. Her husband became the garden's first director. Britton published more than 340 scientific papers. She has had many moss species named after her.

Britton died in the Bronx, New York, when she was 74 years old.

Kansas

Carver followed some neighbors who were moving to Fort Scott, Kansas. He did whatever he could do to earn money. When he had money, he went to school. When he ran out of money, he worked. He faced a great deal of racial **prejudice** at this time.

Carver lived with the Seymours in Olathe, Kansas. Lucy Seymour taught him how to iron ruffles and **pleats** on fancy clothes. He moved with them to Minneapolis, Kansas. He finished high school there.

In 1890, Carver became a high school graduate. He applied to Highland College in Kansas. When he arrived to **register** for school, he was rudely turned away. The college did not accept black students. This was a bad blow for Carver.

Fashion of the time was complex with many details. Ironing such garments, as Carver did, would have been complicated work.

⬆ Suet is made from beef fat. Carver used it to flavor his cornbread.

Art or Science?

Carver became friends with a white couple. They lived in Winterset, Iowa. They encouraged Carver to apply to college again. They saw his **potential.** They believed in him. Carver enrolled at Simpson College in 1890. He was going to study art.

After paying his tuition, Carver only had 10 cents left. For one month, he lived on beef **suet** and corn meal.

Carver's teachers didn't want him to study art. They didn't think he could earn a living with it. The art director saw that Carver had a natural way with plants. She suggested he study **botany**. Botany is the science of plants. Carver stayed at the college for less than a year. Then he transferred to Iowa State. He went there to study agricultural science.

Winner!

Carver entered a drawing contest at the Chicago World's Fair in 1892. He won an honorable mention for his painting of a yucca plant.

Katherine Esau (1898–1997)

Katherine Esau was a pioneering plant **anatomist**. Anatomists study how living things are put together. She was possibly the greatest plant anatomist of the 20th century. She wrote the books *Plant Anatomy* and *Anatomy of Seed Plants*. They are still considered the most important books on plants ever written.

Esau was born in the Ukraine. She was born to a **Mennonite** family. Her father was the mayor of their city. Esau learned to read and write before even starting school. She studied Russian, German, and English. She took piano lessons and went to a gardening school. After her first year of college, she had to move to Germany because of the Russian Revolution.

When Esau was in her 20s, her family moved to America. They went to a town in California. It was near Fresno. Esau first found work as a housekeeper. Then she found work in a seed company. From there, she moved to Davis, California, where she worked and continued her studies.

Later, she settled in Santa Barbara, California. She bought her first computer at the age of 86. She had to take lessons to use it! When Esau was 91 years old, she received the National Medal of Science. Esau died at the age of 99.

College Life

Life at Iowa State was not easy for Carver. He was the first black person to attend the college. He was not allowed to live in the dormitories. They were only for the white students. He slept in an old office. He had to eat in the basement of the dining hall. That's where all the employees ate.

Carver had many struggles. Despite it all, he excelled in school. He learned about how **pollen** works in plants. He also learned about **crossbreeding** plants. This could create new and better breeds of plants and flowers.

Carver also learned how to apply science to farming. He studied soil **composition.** He learned how the nutrients in the soil affect how plants grow.

Living Things on His Jacket

Carver always wore a wrinkled, shabby suit. But he also always had a flower or a piece of evergreen on his jacket lapel.

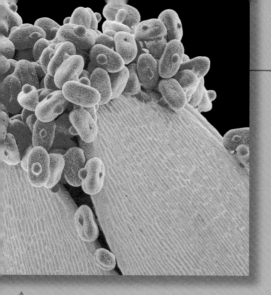

cornflower pollen

Farmers must understand soil and its nutrients in order to grow healthy crops.

David Grandison Fairchild (1869–1954)

David Grandison Fairchild was born in Michigan. He studied agriculture. After his studies, he joined the U.S. Department of Agriculture. He worked there as a botanist and a plant explorer.

Fairchild searched the world for plants that could be brought to America. He introduced more than 80,000 species and varieties of plants to the United States. He brought cherry trees from Japan. He also introduced pistachios, nectarines, bamboo, and avocados.

Fairchild married the daughter of Alexander Graham Bell. They had two children. When he retired, his family settled in Coconut Grove, Florida. He worked to establish a national park in the Everglades.

Professional Life

Carver graduated from Iowa State. Then he earned his master's degree. He had many job offers.

Booker T. Washington invited Carver to Alabama. Washington was a former slave. He was also the driving force in creating the Tuskegee Negro Normal Institute. The school taught **academic** classes to black students. It also taught practical subjects.

Washington asked Carver to join the faculty of the school and to create an agricultural department. Washington believed it was important for black people to be **self-sufficient.** He wanted them to own land. He also wanted to help farmers work their land better.

Carver arrived in Tuskegee. He noticed the cotton crops there were small and sickly. He saw the land was **barren**. It was **eroded.** He planned to teach the farmers better planting and growing techniques. He knew they needed to grow other crops.

Tuskegee Negro Normal School in Alabama

Booker T. Washington

Tuskegee Classes

The classes at Tuskegee were very interesting. They included things such as farming, carpentry, and brickmaking. They also included shoemaking, printing, and cabinetmaking.

Carver found many ways to make useful things out of plants.

No Resources Again

When Carver arrived at the school, the agriculture building was not finished. He had to teach in a shack. It had no heat. Carver had no supplies except for his microscope. It had been a gift from his friends at Iowa State. He needed equipment to teach. So, he sent his students to search for things from the community to use in his laboratory. Carver believed it was important to save everything and to waste nothing.

The Tuskegee Institute was located on an abandoned **plantation.** The land was swampy, with a lot of trash. The land didn't have much grass, flowers, or shrubs. The soil was mostly dry clay. Not much grew there. Carver and his students cleaned up the land. They prepared it for planting healthy crops.

Carver and his students put together their own laboratory.

What Is Chemurgy?

Carver pioneered research in **chemurgy** (KEM-ur-jee). This is the field of science that uses agricultural products for industry.

Who Invented Peanut Butter?

Peanut butter has been invented and reinvented many times in history. Dr. John Harvey Kellogg patented a "Process of Preparing Nut Meal" in 1895. He used peanuts. Carver's research on the peanut began in 1880. So, he is sometimes credited with the invention.

A Great Teacher and a Movable School

Carver didn't agree with the way most students were taught science. They listened to lectures. They read books and learned vocabulary. But they didn't really understand plants.

Carver believed in hands-on learning. His students learned by working outdoors. They did **experiments**. He took his students on nature walks. He showed things to them.

Carver wanted to teach in the community. Farmers needed help. He wanted to go to the farmers. Carver created a movable school. His students built it inside the **Jesup Wagon**. It was like a motor home. It was donated by a man named Morris K. Jesup to help the school. The students drove it to the farms. From it, Carver taught the most recent techniques in farming.

 Carver's "movable school"

Emma Lucy Braun

(1889–1971)

Emma Lucy Braun was born in Cincinnati, Ohio. Her parents were teachers. They encouraged her to appreciate the woodlands. Braun earned three degrees from the University of Cincinnati. She earned her doctorate in botany.

Braun had a sister named Annette. Annette was a **zoologist**. She was the first woman to earn a doctorate from the University of Cincinnati. The sisters were research partners. In the 1940s, the sisters moved together to a house on two acres in the woods. This is where Emma Braun lived for 30 years.

After her retirement from teaching at the university, Emma Braun continued to write and explore. She and her sister would wander the countryside. They would look for interesting or unusual plants. They found many new things throughout Ohio. Braun also worked to save natural areas and to create nature preserves.

Help for the Hard Times

Carver's help to the community included pamphlets for farmers.

Help for the Hard Times

Important to Farmers
Take Note

The Peanut Man

Carver found over 300 uses for the peanut. People called him "The Peanut Man." The following is a list of some of the things he created from the peanut.

- chili sauce
- mock meats
- plum punch
- cosmetic substitutes
- oleo margarine
- paper
- glue
- **linoleum**
- axle grease
- wallboard
- cloth dye

- instant coffee
- mayonnaise
- **laxatives**
- asparagus
- fuel briquettes
- gasoline
- insecticides
- plastics
- ink
- wood stains
- rubber

Carver used many different techniques to turn peanut plants into useful products.

Carver could have made a lot of money from his discoveries. But he believed God inspired and guided his work. He believed his discoveries belonged to the people. He did not want his creations patented. He only applied for three patents during his lifetime.

Corn Plastic

Another plant that has many uses is corn. Did you know that corn can be used to make plastic? It is **renewable** and can degrade over time.

What can be made from corn plastic? Items include trash bags, shopping bags, plastic cups, and disposable eating utensils. Even packing peanuts, golf tees, and ski tickets are sometimes made from corn plastic. You might even be listening to your favorite music on a player made from corn plastic! In the 1980s, electronics industry leaders began using such plastic for the faces of their products. So, today the music of Korn can be played through corn-based plastic. How corny is that?

The Wizard of Tuskegee

Other people wanted Carver to work with them. Thomas Edison was an inventor. He wanted Carver to work for him. He offered Carver a six-figure salary. That was an unbelievable sum of money at the time! Carver turned down the job offer, though.

The carmaker Henry Ford was also interested in Carver. He needed sources for rubber in America. He needed rubber for tires and other car materials. Carver would not leave Tuskegee.

Carver stayed at Tuskegee until he died in 1943. He never married. He was dedicated to his work.

Carver's work changed science forever. Before Carver did his research, almost no one used plant materials. They were only used for food and clothing. Much more scientific advancement has been made because of Carver's creative approach to agriculture.

Inventor

Carver invented synthetic rubber. He also made material for paving highways. He did this from his research on the sweet potato and the pecan.

Geobiologist: Hope Jahren

John Hopkins University

Time Traveler

To understand ancient plants, Hope Jahren collects plant fossils and brings them back to her lab. There, she studies them using microscopes and other tools. Her research tells us about the air, soil, and water that the plants lived in. All these clues help Jahren understand what the climate was like long ago. And maybe how the climate will change in the future.

Jahren is often able to work out of doors, looking for and observing ancient life signs.

▲ Fossils like this one are one way of learning about life long ago.

What was our planet like 45 million years ago? "This was a very different Earth," Jahren says. For one thing, huge trees grew near the North Pole. It wasn't icy back then, but it was still dark six months a year. If you put your houseplants in a dark closet for that long, they will die. So how did a forest survive? Stay tuned. Jahren is on the case.

Experts Tell Us . . .

How surprising is it to find that huge trees survived those long, dark winters near the North Pole? "This is like finding a human being that could live underwater," Jahren says.

Being There

"Working together is a huge part of science," Jahren says. "It's like you're part of a family that's trying to find things out."

Think About

As a kid, Jahren didn't think she would become a scientist. She wanted to be a teacher, doctor, nurse, lawyer, or maybe a writer. What have you thought of becoming?

4 U 2 Do

"I love comic books," Jahren says. She's even drawn comics starring a weasel that's a scientist. Try drawing a comic about something you like to do.

Lab: Transportation Within Plants

We can't see plants grow because they grow so slowly. We do know that plants drink water and nutrients from the earth. Otherwise, they would wilt and die.

To learn more about plants, do an experiment to prove that water is transported from the roots, up the stalk, and out to the leaves of a plant.

Materials

- beaker
- water
- red food coloring
- stalk of celery

Procedure

1 Fill a large glass or beaker with water and add red food coloring until it is dark red.

2 Place the stalk of celery into the beaker and allow it to sit for a while.

3 After some time, the red water will flow through the plant and turn the tips of the leaves red.

4 Peel off one stalk and slice it in half. You will see the small tubes that carry water and nutrients to the leaves.

Conclusion

1 Describe what you observe in the celery. Why do you think you see what you see?

2 What do you think would happen if you turned the stalk upside down and placed the leaves in the colored water? Why?

Glossary

abolitionist—person who wants to abolish, or get rid of, slavery

academic—regular school subjects, i.e., math, English, history, science

agriculture—the science, art, and business of cultivating soil, producing crops, and raising livestock; farming

anatomist—a person who studies the physical structure of plants or animals

barren—unable to produce plants or fruit

botanist—a scientist who studies plants

botany—the scientific study of plants

chemurgy—the use of agricultural products for commercial or industrial use

composition—the way something is made

crop rotation—a method of farming where a number of different plants are grown one after the other on a field so that the earth stays healthy and fertile

crossbreeding—to breed new strains of plants or animals

eroded—worn away

experimented—tested in order to learn something, or to discover whether something works or is true

geobiologist—a scientist who specializes in geology and biology

Jesup Wagon—large vehicle used by Carver to teach school while visiting farms

laxatives—something that helps a person have a bowel movement

linoleum—a tough, washable floor covering

Mennonite—a member of an Anabaptist church characterized particularly by simplicity of life and pacifism

midwife—a person, usually a woman, who is trained to assist women in childbirth

nutrients—nourishment

plantation—large estate or farm, usually in the South, where crops were grown

pleats—folds in cloth, set into place

pollen—a powdery substance made by flowering plants for fertilizing other plants

potential—the possibility of something happening in the future

prejudice—an irrational hatred, fear, or mistrust of a person or group

register—to put information, especially your name, into an official list or record

renewable—a resource, such as lumber, that can be renewed as quickly as it is used up so that it will not run out

segregated—keeping people from different groups separated from one another

self-sufficient—to be able to make enough money or grow enough food to live without having to rely on others

specimen—something that serves as an example

suet—hard fatty tissue around the kidneys of cattle and sheep, used in cooking

timberland—an area of land with woods that can be cut down and sold as lumber

zoologist—a specialist in the branch of biology dealing with animals

Index

Sally Ride Science™ is an innovative content company dedicated to fueling young people's interests in science. Our publications and programs provide opportunities for students and teachers to explore the captivating world of science—from astrobiology to zoology. We bring science to life and show young people that science is creative, collaborative, fascinating, and fun.